"Never Try to Teach a Pig to Sing . . ."

Wit & Wisdom For Leaders

by Donald E. Walker, Ph.D.

"NEVER TRY TO TEACH A PIG TO SING..."
Wit & Wisdom For Leaders
      by Donald E. Walker, Ph.D.

Library of Congress Catalog Card Number: 96-94124
International Standard Book Number: 0-9651194-2-4

TABLE OF CONTENTS

MAKING IT WORK

No one ever became a ball player by walking after the ball. —Vernon Law, former pitcher for the Pittsburgh Pirates 15

The name of the game is bubble up, not hammer down. 17

Getting along in administration is like getting along on a snake farm. 21

There isn't anyone who doesn't count. 23

Nice guys finish last. 25

The biggest learning disability is knowing all the answers. 27

Happiness is an inside job. 29

The child of fear is the father of evil. 31

The owl of Minerva flies at dusk. 33

The great American game is not baseball, it's politics. 35

PERSONAL EFFECTIVENESS

Trust in Allah, but tie your camel. 41

Don't make any solution part of your skin. 43

You can't wag your tail at everyone. 45

Incoming traffic has the right of way in the john. 47

Flattery is like perfume, it's okay to sniff it but don't swallow it. 49

Don't be a smart ass. 51

The debit column is toward the window. 53

Never eat more than you can lift. —Miss Piggy's diet 55

Join the KMA club. 57

Remember. 59

"Who's responsible?" is often the least important question. 61

TEAM WORK

We're in the gig together so let's just settle down and steal each other's songs.
    —Willie Nelson 67

Let people skin their own skunks. 69

We want freedom from above and obedience from below. 71

The trouble with teams is that only the lead dog gets a change in scenery.
     —Sergeant Preston of the Yukon 73

For God so loved the world that he did not send a committee. 75

CREDIT & BLAME

There is no limit to what you can get done if it doesn't matter who gets the
     credit. 81

Victory has a hundred fathers and defeat is an orphan. —John F. Kennedy 83

The person who explains the problem owns the problem. 85

We work for bigger OH'S. 87

Compliment people on a job well done only on days ending in "y." 89

RESENTMENT & REPRISAL

A leader draws twenty percent of his or her pay for being a bedpan. 95

You can never get even with the world. It takes too long and too many
    lawyers. Woody Allen 99

Never get in a shouting match with a damn fool. Someone may walk in and not
    know which one is the damn fool. 101

While there's death, there's hope. 103

Don't kill the messenger. 105

Never go to war on someone else's anger. 107

The road to good intentions is paved with hell. 109

There is always someone who has asbestos underwear. 111

A good heart doesn't help in poker. 113

Wipe your finger before you point to my spots. 115

Therapeutic murders are overrated. 117

You can't go around shooting everybody that annoys you. You could wind up
    alone. —Detective Sergeant Fish, The *Barney Miller* Show 119

STRATEGY

Never try to teach a pig to sing, it wastes your time and it irritates the pig. 125

6

Always give your adversary an honorable path of retreat. 127

Confront unreasonable people with unreasonable people. 129

Don't be afraid to show your back-up lights. 131

Prepare the distaff and God will send the flax. —Margaret Mead's favorite
    proverb. 133

If you are going to run with the big dogs, you have to tinkle on tall trees. 135

Keep a rudder in the water not a paddle. 137

People decide what they want by deciding first what they don't want. 139

TIMING

There is a difference between impatience and importance. 145

The path of later leads to the house of never. 147

Grab fortune by the forelock; he is bald behind. — Latin proverb 149

SURVIVAL

Don't go mountain climbing with your beneficiary. 155

If you wouldn't be pleased to see it on the front page of tomorrow's paper,
    don't do it. 157

You can't always stay in the shallow end. 161

If you have to have an answer now, the answer is NO! 163

If your hair is on fire, don't try to put it out with a hammer. 165

Bedfellows make strange politics. 167

There is truth in wine. 171

Hansel and Gretel were right. 173

Rumps in and horns out didn't save the buffalo. 177

Don't negotiate when you have to go to the bathroom. 179

Every leader has a few silver bullets. 181

Don't let someone else learn to shave on your beard. 183

When they're after you, they're after you. 185

COMMUNICATION

Don't give cashmere answers to burlap questions. 191

Sticks and stones can break your bones, but words can do permanent
damage. — Movie Disk Jockey 193

Truth lives at the bottom of the well. 195

No one acts as tough as he talks. 197

Listen. 199

Confidential is something that you discuss with one person at a time. 201

There is a difference between a horse chestnut and a chestnut horse. 205

PERCEPTIONS

We see only what we look for. We look for only what we know. 211

Enter houses through their doors. 215

It is better to trust too much than too little. 217

We're standing on the edge of an abscess. —Sam Goldwyn 219

"Perhaps, when we've mutated the genes and integrated the neurons and refined the biochemistry, our descendants will come to see us as we see Pooh: frail and slow in logic, weak in memory and pale in abstraction, but usually warmhearted, generally compassionate, and on occasion possessed of innate common sense and uncommon perception."

-Robert Sinsheimer, *TIME*, April 19, 1971

MAKING IT WORK

Here is Edward Bear, coming downstairs now, bump, bump, bump, on the back of his head, behind Christopher Robin. It is, as far as he knows, the only way of coming downstairs, but sometimes he feels that there really is another way, if only he could stop bumping for a moment and think of it.

A. A. Milne
Winnie-the-Pooh

No one ever became a ball player by walking after the ball.
—Vernon Law, former pitcher for the Pittsburgh Pirates

This is a proverb that applies not only to baseball, but to life in general. A high level of energy and drive make things happen. High motivation and extra effort have a pretty good chance of producing results. What Dr. Paul Saltzman says about exercise applies to organizations also. "You can't get something for nothing. In fact, you can't even break even." The person whose management position has simply turned into a "I dislike apathy, but what the hell" holding action may have outlived his or her usefulness to the organization.

Another meaning can be wrung from this axiom. "Try to learn something new about the job or about people every day." (People are at the heart of everything.) We never stand still. We go a bit backward or forward every day.

The name of the game is bubble up, not hammer down.

The work force has changed. In the morning of this century the assembly line took a largely unskilled, immigrant measled work force, many of whom could not even read and write, and turned them into working teams that gave the American labor force the highest standard of living in the world without sacrificing freedom. Hurray!

The worker today is better educated than the worker was in the early days of this century, more individualistic and, contrary to the stereotype, committed to hard work when the work is interesting and meaningful. Most do not long to go to Tahiti and paint.

There is a lot of talent out there, but it must be conjured. It cannot be effectively commanded. The job of the leader is to create atmospheres in which this talent is called forth. Someone once observed of the Mayo Clinic,

"It is an organization that enables ordinary doctors to practice extraordinary medicine." This captures the idea exactly.

Agendas can be clear. Goals can be lofty. Regulations can be reasonable and tight. Patty cake administration doesn't make it, but the work place isn't a plantation either. Organizations work best when the organization chart doesn't look like a pyramid, but more like a web, or a grid, or a team.

"The beginner sees many possibilities, the expert few. Be a beginner every day."

-Zen

Getting along in administration is like getting along on a snake farm.

Getting along as a leader in an organization involves the same strategies as getting along on a snake farm. Keep moving but don't make sudden, jerky movements. Nobody likes surprises.

The endless trial ballooning in Washington is necessary. The general rule is, "Tell them what you're going to do, tell them what you're doing and tell them what you did." Orthodontial strategies are the most desirable and healing — turn the wire gradually. You can't jerk organizations, or the people in them, around.

There isn't anyone who doesn't count.

This insight is at the heart of democracy and all the great religions — "Not a sparrow shall fall . . ." Sometimes it's hard to remember that it's really true — that people are at the center. It is especially true in a democracy, and in the better organizations, on this, the third planet from the sun, in the last decade of the twentieth century.

The negative side of that equation, long known to politicians, is that "people not strong enough to elect you may be strong enough to defeat you." As the television comedian reminds us, "If you don't think one person can make a difference, light a cigar on an airliner!"

Nice guys finish last.

That statement may be okay if it comes from Dr. Ruth or Masters and Johnson, but it's a lousy and unrealistic view for leaders. Being a nice person doesn't mean you always have to be liked or that the balance sheet is unimportant. But no organization works well when the scenario is survival of the fittest in a basket of crabs world — where the rule is "weakest to the wall."

Someone has said, "Administrators are either tin men or straw men. If they have a brain, they don't have a heart." Maybe in the land of Oz, but that's a fairy tale.

The problem can run deeper than the cynicism of the quote. It somehow implies a morally shabby world where any action can be justified to get ahead. The records of the most successful companies in the country, examined carefully, are proof that such a view is full of digested hay.

The biggest learning disability is knowing all the answers.

Knowing all the answers is a way of nailing the box shut from inside. The ancients had another word for it — hubris — overweening pride. Hubris was the sin that the gods punished most consistently.

In a world where things are changing so rapidly to assume the answers are obvious is, as Pogo says, "Ridicledockle."

Of course, seeking consultation can itself become a pathology, but exploring all the alternatives and accepting other readily available perspectives from knowledgeable people is an absolutely fundamental exercise in today's world. This is not just a "kindergarten" fact of leadership. In this instance, we're talking "day care."

Happiness is an inside job.

In an art museum I once saw a painting entitled simply "Flower Garden." As one approaches the canvas, a little girl is seen on her hands and knees on the asphalt of a city street in a defeated little dress drawing flowers with a piece of white chalk. Our flower gardens are inside.

The job of leadership is to keep the soil rich and nourished so that flowers can grow. Our charter isn't broad enough to take charge of someone's interior climate. The leader who extravagantly expends time and energy in the attempt to plump someone up like a sofa cushion will meet with disappointment. That person can always say to themselves or others, "Not soon enough" or "not far enough." "Have a good day is not the eleventh commandment." After all the world isn't perfect. Everything has lumps.

The job of the leader is to fix destinations, to solve problems, to preserve values, to create climates in which able people can and want to give their best. The most successful leader sets an example. Certainly that's enough to expect of anyone.

The child of fear is the father of evil.

Old time movies often portrayed a boss who liked to shout at people just to make their laundry bills go up. Not many decades ago, there was an assumption running through management literature that fear was the ultimate agent of control, the final coordinator of effort when the goody, goody stuff failed. The often unspoken premise was that the attempt to run an organization by teamwork, loyalty and fair play was too fragile to be relied upon. Such views, while rare, are not unexampled in these more sophisticated and complicated times.

Fear may work as the primary agent of control for a period, particularly in highly structured organizations with a paramilitary chain of command accepted or imposed. Except in times of great crisis it doesn't wear well. When people are genuinely frightened, they do desperate and unpredictable things and that's not good for the organization or the people in it including leaders. The feared dictators of history are almost without exception overtaken by nemesis. "The mills of the gods grind slowly, but they grind exceeding fine."

The owl of Minerva flies at dusk.

In classic mythology Minerva's owl was the symbol of wisdom. The ancients noticed that as we get older we get wiser. Intelligence tests don't measure wisdom. Somehow that is an add on, an effervescence, an intangible that is difficult to quantify.

Leaders can use the accumulated wisdom and the subtle, refined judgments of older workers. As the saying goes "youth for sail, age for rudder." Unfortunately as people gather years, they are not equally wise in all areas. It takes careful conversation and exploration to use people's strengths while minimizing their weaknesses.

It's too easy to dismiss older workers as over age salmon trying to climb the dam. But, in these days of a ripening population, it's worth the effort to keep older people in the work force perhaps on flexible schedules. In paraphrase of Robert Frost, a good part of life is "hanging around long enough to catch on." And as Alice Roosevelt Longsworth once noted, "The secret of eternal youth is arrested development."

The great American game is not baseball, it's politics.

There is a lot of political behavior going on in organizations. By political behavior I mean:

1.   Power is divided. It really is. It's impossible to run a big organization entirely from the front office.

2.   Often the people at the bottom of the "chain of command" have more authority to decide what will happen than the people at the top. Whether, for example, the new bonding machine will work smoothly or develop all kinds of glitches often depends not on the supervisor but on the operator of the machine.

3.   We work with the consent of those we supervise—not approval, consent. Consent means that even though not everyone likes what we are doing, they'll go along.

4. We personalize resentment, we blame people for problems, no matter how complicated those problems are. The charges levied are intemperate. "Crooked enough to wear orthopedic underwear." "Enough mouth for an extra row of teeth." "Dumb as a pool float." The list is endless.

5. Most organizations are political in that people often decide what they want by deciding first what they don't want. A proposal is made, there is opposition and then if the place is running right, a compromise occurs. It can be frustrating, but coalitions, teams, networks, whatever term you use, often get more accomplished than individual Tarzans swinging from tree to tree.

    The process is not as tidy or antiseptic as it may seem. Most of this compromise and coalition building is the end result of struggle over limited resources. Most of us are not comfortable with conflict.

Leaders must learn to accept it as "normal" and to manage it creatively rather than simply trying to stamp it out which never works.

6.   The instincts of organizations in a free society are deeply democratic. Companies that haven't learned this are often plagued by strikes, low morale and absenteeism.

This doesn't mean that they are democracies and that everybody votes or that every issue is voted upon.

PERSONAL EFFECTIVENESS

"Her feet are too big. Her nose is too long. Her teeth are uneven. She has the neck, as one of her rivals put it, of "a Neapolitan giraffe." Her waist seems to begin in the middle of her thighs, and she has big, half-bushel hips. She runs like a fullback. Her hands are huge. Her forehead is low. Her mouth is too large. And, *mamma mia*, she is absolutely gorgeous."

TIME, April 6, 1962 (From a story on Sophia Loren when she won an Academy Award for the film, <u>Two Women</u>.)

Trust in Allah, but tie your camel.

This is a statement out of the scripture of the Middle East that goes back over fifteen hundred years.

There is a deep meaning for leaders in the proverb.

Leaders bear responsibility for caution and for extra effort, including the need to remind people. A case in point: An aide to Jack Kennedy once observed that the President spent much of his time on the telephone reminding people of assignments or "renewing the pressure." If the president of the United States has to keep prodding associates, how can we escape? Remember: "Even when you've got it in the bag, you ain't got it in the bag." "The problem of non-compliance is as old as Adam and Eve."

It doesn't work to simply throw ourselves on the world and expect things to turn out right. On the prairie frontier, a similar idea was expressed in the exhortation, "Pray to heaven for a good harvest, and then hoe like hell."

Don't make any solution part of your skin.

Remember the goal is to solve problems. Often a leader's proposed solution will call forth suggestions for modification or even a totally different strategy. The leader to be perceived as a leader doesn't have to be the parent of every idea. For good people to propose alternatives is healthy and part of a natural process. Some of these proposals will be better than the original.

The sometime reluctance of a leader to accept alternate solutions often derives from the notion that there is a perfect battering ram for every barricade, a perfect resolution for every problem, a perfect balm for every injury — not true. Everything in life is a trade off, a compromise. Everything has a price tag, but often what you lose on the peanuts you make up on the popcorn.

You can't wag your tail at everyone.

The desire to please is one that's built deeply into our society. We are social animals. It may be even part of our genetic structure. Leaders are stuck. No decision will please everyone. As a university president once remarked, "If you want approval, get a puppy."

I've heard leaders say, "I don't want to be loved, I'd rather be respected." That, too, is a threadbare hope. When people don't like you, they find reasons not to respect you.

Leaders must either consult a nourishing inner oracle or admiring friends to fill this need. Excessive efforts by a leader to be liked in the work place are received like a request for a light at the American Cancer Society.

Incoming traffic has the right of way in the john.

Human beings share the fundamental urges, but the intensity of need varies from person to person, and from time to time. One person's need for a desk near a window may be so intense that working in a closed room may completely destroy his or her efficiency. Another person may need no breaks at all or only one short break in the afternoon. Another may be willing to work overtime, and may be a tremendous producer, but needs frequent short breaks. Everyone needs to be complimented, but at a particular time the need in someone may subvert all others.

The best leaders have a sensitivity to such urgencies.

This proverb may be valenced to include irritations. The need to remedy small annoyances is just as important as the filling of small but urgent needs. "More trees are killed by bugs than by lightning."

Flattery is like perfume, it's okay to sniff it but don't swallow it.

The higher one ascends in the organizational balloon, the funnier his or her jokes become and the wiser his or her counsel seems to be. This does not mean that every smile should be polygraphed. People are largely sincere in laughing at the boss's jokes and paying close attention to his or her opinions. After all, when things are going well, people like to think of those in authority over them as competent and sensible.

But, don't get peacock fever. Remember it's not all just wonderful you. That recognition does not come as easily as one might think. A little cynicism isn't enough protection. Such reinforcement is addictive and oh, so fragrant, but it often disappears with the position. Many a CEO, accustomed to having people permit the president to go through the door first, goes to a convention out of town and finds that he or she has a tendency to bump into people in doorways.

Don't be a smart ass.

Every leader is tempted to use karate chop putdowns, at least once in a while. Wouldn't it be great to answer a surly remark by saying: "When I want any crap out of you, I'll kick it out." or "You'd make a wonderful neighbor for someone who has a windmill." or "My, you'd make a great pinata." or "Don't you have to go somewhere and shed your skin." or "Isn't it sad when cousins marry." or "I hope you and your marbles are reunited." or "Are you off your medication again?" or "I hope Santa brings you what you need most, toilet paper." It would provide great satisfaction to send back some snotty memo with the note: "Some jackass has been sending out letters like this and signing your name. I thought you should know."

Those are wonderful replies that ought to have a home in some brilliant repartee. Just be certain it isn't yours.

Soft words go down more easily when you have to eat them. Whether they know the proverb or not, many people are familiar with the notion that "There's truth in anger." Smart ass comments will be remembered by everyone, including the boss — remember the old admonition — if you are going to kick the king, you had better kill him.

The debit column is toward the window.

The cynical story is that when the Lord conferred upon Solomon the gift of wisdom, in the blinding transfiguring instant that the gift was bestowed, Solomon realized that he should have wished for money.

The leader should learn more about finances than that the debit column is toward the window. Leaders often have charismatic and interpersonal skills which are more critical in carrying them to positions of prominence than awareness of the balance sheet. Financial expertise seems to be more the province of technicians than of leaders. Nevertheless, when the vice president for business says to the president, "We can't afford it," the president has to know whether that is a sound fiscal judgment or a preference. Leaders must learn where the money goes, and where it can be hidden. You don't have to be a CPA to develop good instincts about financing. A good money nose is essential.

Never eat more than you can lift.
—Miss Piggy's diet

Paying attention to dietary imports and exports is a necessity for everyone, but particularly for leaders working in high stress positions. Growing an important stomach is not a sign of success. The admonition should also be read as more than "avoid road kill chili at eleven o'clock at night." Pay attention to <u>all</u> the rules of health is the formulae. An apple a day doesn't make it.

There is a deeper meaning to the proverb. Miss Piggy's advice applies to administrative plans as well. The advice can be read as not to undertake more than you can handle. That injunction goes down a bit lumpy. Our notions of leadership are heroic. We have a model in our heads of the muscle manager, the Gary Cooper sheriff who ties his gun down, stands in the middle of the road and fights his way through. Fortunately, the designated driver within us knows that the scenario isn't terribly realistic. I remember a discussion with a general in the United States Army. I asked him what was the secret of becoming a successful general. He replied, "Never give an order that won't be obeyed." Even so, leaders differ from commanders. The roles are not the same.

Join the KMA club.

K stands for kiss. The leader who is worried continually about keeping his position will be severely handicapped. The leader who prepares alternative strategies, builds up a cash reserve, and accepts invitations for job interviews will, on balance, do a better job wherever he or she is. There is nothing as risky as always playing it safe. There are times in life when you have to work without a net.

Remember.

"The injunction, 'Thou shalt not kill' occurs once in the Bible. The exhortation 'Remember' over a hundred times." Remember to praise, remember to say thank you, remember to apologize, remember to think ahead, remember to plan, remember to be on time, remember names, remember to remember.

Leaders with good memories who work at it in subtle and difficult to quantify ways do strikingly better than people who think "Others are paid to remind me. My job is to get the job done."

"Who's responsible?" is often the least important question.

The question "Who is responsible?" implies that people work alone but in a chain of command.

I remember reading an account of a college president, who one morning was confronted by a room full of upset students because young trees on campus had been cut down. The campus was admittedly "urban and ugly." In response, the President, a person of high natural wattage, nevertheless called a meeting of top administrators to find out "who was responsible?" He never found "the" villain. The probable reason was that we are often accomplices to one another. In a bureaucratic organization the decision to cut trees was doubtless a shared one, necessary in order to carry out another decision such as the one to build a loading dock for the student union.

If the incident had caused so much concern, instead of using administrative time and talent trying to find a villain, the meeting should have been called to plan the planting of more trees.

In the best organizations people work with one another to help solve problems and to steady a faltering performer so that everyone looks good and there are more profits to share. An attitude of "we are physicians to one another" is a perspective to be treasured.

Another advantage to such a problem solving approach is that if there is on the team a person who is truly inadequate, then other members of the work team often play a role in encouraging that person to resign or accept transfer to a different assignment.

"One way to get along in a bureaucracy is to pretend it doesn't exist and let it adjust to you."

-Anonymous

TEAM WORK

"Of course he doesn't discriminate. He treats us all the same — like dogs."

-Player for Vince Lombardi

We're in the gig together so let's just settle down and steal each other's songs. —Willie Nelson

We're all in the same world. We need and depend on one another. As the anonymous poet reminds us,

> "I have drunk from wells
> I did not dig.
> I have been warmed by fires
> I did not build."

Even when we feel like loners, unremembered voices comfort us and unseen hands touch us. There is a lesson here for work teams.

Lefty Gomez was once asked the secret of being a great pitcher and he replied, "Clean living and a fast outfield." Certainly, in today's world, team play is the name of the game. We've known for years, perhaps centuries, that people involved in difficult decisions are more committed to those decisions, have higher morale and will work harder to see that things turn out right than when they are simply "carrying out orders."

Let people skin their own skunks.

The boss who bellows, "Don't bring me problems; bring me solutions" may not just be trying to make his job easier. Good leaders summon talent and accept solutions from everyone in the organization. It's more than a matter of command however. The challenge is to get people's skins into the game so that they not only solve their own problems but contribute to problem solving teams, rather than ducking and complaining.

In all organizations, from time to time, it's tempting for leaders to "put the wet baby in someone else's lap." It's easy to view every problem as someone else's responsibility. Where the boss feels that central casting put other people on earth just to make him or her look good, ducking is common. No one cares to be a bit actor in that scenario.

An additional advantage of encouraging people to solve their own problems is that you get better solutions. As W.C. Fields remarked, "If you want to know about juggling, ask a juggler."

We want freedom from above
and obedience from below.

The difficulty is with the concept of pyramid. It started with the German sociologist Max Weber. The idea of the hierarchy as the most efficient kind of organization for non-military bureaucracies was bolted onto the American civil service system by Woodrow Wilson. It spread. Observed more in the breach than in the performance, it is now clearly dysfunctional. The CEO is no longer at the apex of a pyramid but more the center of a circle where "communication is more important than command." The only way to respond to the thirst for simultaneous freedom from above and obedience from below is to operate in team and networking styles and in non-pyramidal ways.

The trouble with teams is that only the lead dog gets a change in scenery. —Sergeant Preston of the Yukon

The proverb reflects the traditional attitude toward work teams as line hitches with a leader at the front and willing helpers in descending rank behind. Successful teams are no longer organized in that fashion. There's an inclusiveness, a feel of "we're all in the game together" about highly effective teams. It's the commitment of championship volleyball competitors. In organizations where everybody feels part of the action and an allegiance to a common goal, a creative synergy occurs.

For God so loved the world that he did not send a committee.

Committees get a bum rap. We are the most social animals on earth. We perform medical and engineering miracles every day by team work — often in committees.

There are real skills to be learned in effectively working with others. We fail to identify and practice them because the rhetoric about committees is unflattering and goes contrary to our macho and individualistic fantasies about how to get things done.

Also, committees can be an acceptable vehicle for avoiding tough decisions as the stereotyped cliches indicate. Statements such as, "If you can't commit yourself, committee yourself" or "A committee is a creature with six or more legs and no head" can be true, but only because leaders do not know how to work with committees and do not lead.

Leaders today must identify and practice the skills required to get the most from teams, committees, task forces or whatever else cooperating groups are called.

Often such learning begins with as simple an act as the leader's willingness to take the blame for failure or mistakes and accept responsibility for final decisions. "I will accept full responsibility for this decision, but I need the best advice I can get in making that decision. You people are experts in your own areas. I need your help."

Again, when things go well, everyone must share the credit.

"One monkey can't stop a show."

-Flip Wilson

CREDIT & BLAME

"It's easier to get forgiveness than permission."

-Bob Lawrence

There is no limit to what you can get done if it doesn't matter who gets the credit.

The most admired leaders in any organization are the ones who spend time and effort pushing the credit on other people. Strangely enough this never seems to diminish their own portion. Try it and see. Sharing of credit is slightly different than paying compliments. To share credit is a kind of compliment in itself, but actively working at praise is a separate but related task.

Victory has a hundred fathers and defeat is an orphan.

—John F. Kennedy

A complicated problem is resolved. The leader feels that he or she has overcome tremendous resistance and the victory clearly belongs to him or her. Then people appear from everywhere explaining how they carried it off. Such events can cause cynicism, but they should not. Success is something that belongs to everyone especially in these days of computer network problem solving. The great military commanders in history have known that victory is plural and made certain that the foot soldiers were recognized and rewarded.

Good organizations can become great when they discover that the secret is to expand the success group. Let everyone own the victory. Forget about finding villains.

A balancing proverb is that, "No one wants to be holding the cookie when it crumbles."

The person who explains the problem owns the problem.

Have you ever noticed on national television when a crisis threatens and someone is making explanations for the State Department or the Army that press questions become increasingly stiletto and the person explaining more defensive? It's a normal human tendency to hold the person explaining responsible.

The student radicals of the 70s tried hard to find individual villains for complicated institutional problems. One of the weapons in their arsenal was summarized by someone, "When you don't know who to talk to, start a fire and talk to the guy who comes out with a hose." Often, the guy with the hose had done nothing to cause the difficulties and could offer no remedies.

Good leaders often alternate the people who do the explaining to keep people's minds on the larger problem rather than the person who is trying to clear things up.

We work for bigger OH'S.

Question: "Where do you work?"

Answer: "I'm a physician." Response: "Oh"

"Actually, I'm a surgeon." "Oh"

"My specialty is neurosurgery." "Oh"

"I'm professor of neurosurgery at the medical school." "Oh"

Titles and status are important as the colleague who voiced this proverb points out. The most applicable lesson for leaders is to confer titles and other status and achievement rewards with care and to be certain that they are related to unusual or outstanding performance. Believe it or not, for many people there are satisfactions in a job that go beyond salary. Past a certain point, for some, salary may be mostly a way of keeping score. Remember, too, that we must receive four times as much praise as criticism before we feel that the two are equal.

Compliment people on a job well done only on days ending in "y."

In every company there are people of great candle power who are loaded with talent and good ideas. One of the surest ways to get them to share this treasure is to cultivate the habit of noticing outstanding performance and rewarding it, usually in nonmonetary ways. I believe it was the CEO of a large cosmetics company who advised, "Walk softly and carry a big carrot."

We neglect that wisdom. I remember seeing a Charlie Brown poster in an office in Washington, D.C. a number of years ago. Charlie was remarking ruefully, "Doing a good job around here is like wetting your pants in a dark suit. It gives you a warm feeling, but nobody notices."

The habit of offering sincere compliments can be harder to develop than it looks. It's an imperfect world, and, in organizations, we fall effortlessly into the habit of criticism. It's easy to notice when colleagues hit the institutional speed bumps. It's not hard to compliment the performance that is absolutely dazzling in its brilliance especially when the performer is not competing for the next promotion; but beyond saluting the obvious pinnacles, compliments often seem to us to be artificial or even Machiavellian. No one wants to be accused of yummying up to the boss or anyone else. After all, nothing is perfect, and part of us wants people to see that we could have done as well or perhaps even better.

Widely practiced, the habit of complimenting colleagues rather than criticizing can change the character of companies or organizations. Reciprocity sets in. As Yogi might have said, "It's mutual on both sides." I remember hearing the story of the president of a small company who turned the organization around using this principle. Every morning he called a brief staff meeting. Each individual present was asked to name the person who had helped him or her most in the previous day. After the opening exercise, the person receiving the highest number of compliments was asked to chair the staff meeting on the following morning. It was a tournament-level idea and it hasn't been patented.

Our tendency is to pay more attention to mistakes than to successes. We remember Icarus and not Daedalus. Daedalus made it.

"The headbone is connected to the heart."

-Alan Alda

RESENTMENT & REPRISAL

"Friends, yes, strangers, I don't know." -Oscar Levant, when asked by an army psychiatrist, "Could you kill?"

A leader draws twenty percent of his or her pay for being a bedpan.

When things go wrong, people need in-residence tyrants. When life is a pain and the organization is playing fiscal bungee, it helps to believe leaders are slippery and stupid. It's a durable quip that "leaders don't have freckles because they slide off." Further, managers are chronically suspected of Fonzie Bear answers. As one department head commented, "We have one supervisor so dumb the other supervisors know it."

The hostility between worker and boss in this country goes back at least to the time of Alex de Tocqueville who remarked on the phenomenon in the early days of the Republic. The recognition of this circumstance may be the parent of the quip, "A raisin is a grape that has been in administration." When we are frustrated, there is little satisfaction in being mad at the company. That's like being mad at the corner of First and Main. When things go wrong (and they do even in the best run organizations), then the leader is going to be the catcher's mitt, if not for hardball hate at least for fast ball resentment.

There are no heroes in tough times. In the words of Archie Bunker, a leader in stressed times will be "popular as baked beans on a bus trip." Jim March reminds us that "strong leaders" come out of good times with suspicious regularity.

When you're the leader in really bad times, people who have known and liked you for years may stop waving at you with all of their fingers. One colleague even complained that someone saluted him with his little finger on the ground that he "didn't even care enough to give his very best."

Again, a colleague complained that most of the time she finds herself between the dog and the tree.

Even so, there are compensating rewards. "*Les Miserables* is not French for leader."

"Ya gotta learn to play hurt."

-Pro football saying

You can never get even with the world. It takes too long and too many lawyers. Woody Allen

Life isn't fair. The caterpillar does all the work, the butterfly gets all the admiration. We don't always get what's coming to us and that is both good and bad news. The acceptance of the fact that the world isn't always fair is in some deep sense the beginning of wisdom. As someone once said, "Expecting the universe to treat you with courtesy and concern because you are a nice person is like expecting the bull not to gore you because you are a vegetarian." Learn to live with life's imperfections, fleas and all. You'll do better, live longer and probably be happier. It is not true that virtue is its <u>only</u> reward.

The advice, "Don't get mad, get even" is unsteady. It poisons the well. The Chinese were wiser centuries ago when they counseled, "Before you set out on the path of revenge, dig two graves."

Leadership responsibility is central. Slap and dodge scenarios often start at the top or tend to flourish when leaders haven't made up their minds about how the place works best.

Never get in a shouting match with a damn fool. Someone may walk in and not know which one is the damn fool.

When you're breathing heavily, breathe through your nose. I'm not saying that temper tantrums are never a permissible tool of management to establish boundaries, to increase alertness, to emphasize the rules. In cases when I've seen a leader throw an effective tantrum, I've always had a strong suspicion that the thrower was really in control and providing theater. An honest to God, out of control temper tantrum is a sign that the individual is unable to cope. That's an interpretation made by everyone. If the leader is well thought of, the organization adjusts to compensate for the behavior and it is forgiven but not forgotten. The incident leaves a callus that is seen as covering a weak spot.

While there's death, there's hope.

It is probably true that any organization of reasonable size would profit from a good funeral or two. After all, no one is perfect and some key person can be a real road block. As a large scale strategy, however, the notion that killing the bad guys and promoting the good guys will solve all the problems is an illusion. Problems are more complicated than that. Leaders sometimes feel that suppressing criticism by getting rid of critics will solve the problem. Wrong. There are always heat-seeking personalities warming up. When one problem tooth is extracted, another tooth becomes sore in its place. The trick in organizations is to get imperfect people to work together for common purposes and, as much as possible and as frequently as feasible, to encourage people to help one another rather than stand in each other's way.

Don't kill the messenger.

Ancient kings frequently killed the messenger who brought them bad news, and criticisms are often received as bad news. Someone once said, "Criticism is difficult to take from a friend, an enemy, an acquaintance, or a stranger."

The first reaction bureaucracies have to criticism is to hunt down the criticizer. Since all complaint is an abstraction and a fraction of the complaint is unfair and wrong, that's seems justification enough for shutting up the critic.

It isn't. Criticism makes a hard pillow, but it is useful — not always correct or, at least, not totally correct but always useful. Try to develop in supervisors and work teams a hospitality to unpleasant news. It's a subtle thing, but where it exists the organization benefits and leaders also reap that benefit.

Never go to war on someone else's anger.

Even the most trusted colleagues see the world through their own glasses. The leader who puts his hand on his gun after listening only to a friend's anger may be premature. He may even be kicking an open door. As the Chinese proverb says, "Remember, the other side has another side." For a leader to adopt uncritically another person's irritation sends a wrong signal to the troops even if the irritation is largely justified. The unjustified ten percent opens up like an umbrella if the fuss continues.

The road to good intentions is paved with hell.

It's always a surprise to leaders when they find themselves criticized or attacked for actions rooted in the most noble motives. That goes in sideways. One leader complained, "When I do something that's really nice, it's only because I'm concerned about my image. When I do something that people don't like, it's because that's my natural way of behaving." Maybe the action criticized was just kind of an extra, an add on, a generosity intended to make life easier or better for someone.

The problem is even more complicated when leaders encounter the tendency to interpret uncharacteristic behavior as that which is closest to basic character. Someone, who is kind and perhaps overattentive to the needs of people, looses his or her temper. It is assumed by some that their basic nature is to be irritable and quick tempered. On the other hand, someone who has justly earned the reputation for being a grouchy, unsympathetic curmudgeon is seen petting a stray dog and that action may be assumed to be closest to the true character of the individual.

In the long term, it sorts. It's just something to be noted not pouted about.

There is always someone who has asbestos underwear.

In every organization there is someone who has protection. One is the son of the boss, another the daughter of the chairman of the board, or someone else owns critical shares of voting stock. Usually these untouchables are not pit bull personalities who make people's lives miserable nor are they even felony stupid. More often than not their work simply isn't quite the quality or quantity that the better people in the organization are putting out. It is a rare occasion when you will have someone on board who can't keep his or her self-winding watch going and couldn't organize a two car funeral.

Leaders shouldn't spend too much time trying to eliminate such people. As the Spanish proverb says, "With the rich and mighty always a little patience." It isn't a perfect world. Learn to work around them is the best advice.

A good heart doesn't help in poker.

People behave differently toward one another in organizational roles than they do one on one. A person who individually is thoughtful, willing to concede ground gracefully in an argument and is attentive to human needs may react quite differently in an organizational setting. It's the difference between interpersonal behavior in a friendly game of checkers as contrasted with a game of high stakes poker. The person who may let a friend win a game of checkers because his morale seems low and he needs a little boost may act differently when there is big money in the pot.

In situations of conflict within an organization, people often react with savagery that seems quite out of keeping with their "normal" personalities. Again the problem lies with the scenarios in their heads. If people feel they are in a contest with unscrupulous, Machiavellian tyrants, intemperate response seems justified. "I know what those bastards are trying to get away with. If they want to play hard ball, I'll play hard ball too" is a familiar speech in times of organizational crisis.

When the interests of a company are perceived as diverging mightily from the interests of the people who work within it, there is trouble.

Wipe your finger before you point to my spots.

People resent most in others the faults that they secretly perceive in themselves. The legendary critic comes to mind who complained that the neighborhood boys were whistling dirty songs.

The guy who is certain that other salesmen are cheating on their expense reports prompts a closer investigation of his own. The department manager who continually and stridently complains that her assistants are not loyal to her hoists a cautionary flag. The person who believes that others are gossips may be seen by others as the leading local distributor of hearsay. A comment by Ralph Waldo Emerson is instructive, "The louder he talked of honor, the faster we counted the spoons."

The opposite side of this truth is that people appreciate in others the virtues they possess themselves often without being aware of strength in the area. This is a key part of the proverb to depend and build on. Making people aware of their strong points puts the iron in them and that's not bad news for anyone.

Therapeutic murders are overrated.

Stressed organizations are not "Mr. Rogers' Neighborhood." A new leader coming in to such a toxic environment will often be presented with a suggestion by a variety of people, "Just twelve more therapeutic murders and this place will be fine." The problem is that nearly everyone in a position of responsibility is on someone's hit list, often each others.

There are other problems with this scenario as anyone who has had leadership experience comes to recognize. In the first place, no one sees himself or herself as a villain. The work place is not one big game of cops and robbers. There are few willing scoundrels in this world. Diabolism is bad causality. Large problems involving numbers of people are frequently structural rather than personal.

The problem can be the way the company is organized and attempts to deal with perceived pathologies. In such situations, changes work best when they are built around the assumption that most people, most of the time, want to do well and only become involved in hostile strategies to protect themselves.

You can't go around shooting everybody that annoys you. You could wind up alone.
—Detective Sergeant Fish, The *Barney Miller* Show

Your proctologist may be the only one who has a license to be a pain in the behind, nevertheless, every leader marching down the hall after a frustrating day has seen a colleague and discovered to his or her surprise that his or her impulse is to grab him by the legs and make a wish.

Anger comes from frustration. Frustration comes with your bellybutton. You have to learn to handle it. The person who can't is on his way to another job or another world.

Regarding the aggravations of existence as problems to be met rather than as unmerited impediments to lofty goals and good intentions is a step in the right direction.

A part of managing our resentments is paying attention to the stories that we use to scaffold reality. As a highly successful writer of children's books once observed, we continually tell ourselves stories. If someone we are to meet on a corner is late, we instantly begin to construct a scenario to explain events. Beginning with, "Something has happened to her" and moving on to "She's forgotten. She didn't even care enough to write it down." When the individual appears with a satisfactory explanation, all the resentment is dissipated and the scaffolding we have built is disassembled.

We dismiss our sunniest stories and anticipations as permissible day dreams. We seldom pay enough attention to our hostile story lines or recognize how frequently they are wrong. Unattended resentments over a considerable period of time can take us out of the gene pool. Our arteries are listening to the stories we tell ourselves.

"He who has a thousand friends has not a friend to spare. And he who has an enemy will meet him everywhere."

Frontier Rhyme

STRATEGY

"You can't beat on the horses and pull back on the reins."

-Ed Walker

Never try to teach a pig to sing, it wastes your time and it irritates the pig.

Some things cannot be changed or else simply are not worth the effort required to do so. As someone once asked, "Did you ever hear of an obedience school for cats?" People who don't want to change probably can't be changed. What leaders can often modify is the way people perceive their work. Whether they see hard work as worth the effort, or whether they regard the work place as fair or unfair, can be influenced. Again, tournament-level leaders spend their efforts creating an environment where good things emerge, in which people are permitted and even encouraged to find their own special place in an organization that is well ordered and concerned with human beings.

Always give your adversary an honorable path of retreat.

When an adversary has been caught dead to rights in a mistake, or an error or even in a plot to embarrass or frustrate, it's wisest to resist the temptation to really hand it to him. Often a statement like "I know you may not have had complete information when you made the decision, but . . ." avoids a bruised ego.

Granting there is a shade within us that rises in the night and whoops around the bonfire and the kill, it's better to keep that part of us under control. As a conquering general once remarked, "You can have revenge, or you can have peace; but you can't have both." It's amazing how even a coward will fight when cornered or how long it takes a wound to heal when someone has been savaged and embarrassed in front of others.

Confront unreasonable people with unreasonable people.

Getting people together in the same room who disagree offers a method of resolving difficulties more quickly and easily than when a third party tries to be peacemaker. Remember the Chinese proverb: "The go-between wears out a thousand sandals."

Often the person who demands that the leader chasten some misbehaving colleague becomes much more reasonable when the leader says, "You make some good points. I understand your indignation. Let's just settle this thing right now by having Smith join us." The rejoiner is often, "Oh, I don't need to be here. I'm sure you can handle it." The reply should be, "No, you've put matters very well. This gives you a chance to get the sand out of your shoes, and I'd like to hear Smith's response."

Such a proposal often results in change of scenario when the offending individual arrives. The rhetoric is less shrill. Reports are more accurate, and the cries for blood less strident. As a colleague advocating this technique remarked, "Both parties to the disagreement leave the room with each holding an arm of that monkey."

Don't be afraid to show your back-up lights.

Question: "But if I change my mind, won't people think that I am weak and can't stick by a decision?" Answer: "You can't wobble around on every issue or sail downstream whichever way the wind is blowing. But if you make a mistake, everybody will know it. To backup and do it again will merely be perceived as flexibility and intelligence rather than weakness or vacillation. At least by most people most of the time. That is far better than embarking on a "love affair with foolishness."

We have the wrong idea about leadership. The notion of the John Wayne, tough guy, who never makes mistakes, never apologizes, who just charges ahead and ultimately saves the wagon train is fiction. Everyone makes mistakes.

Prepare the distaff and God will send the flax. —Margaret Mead's favorite proverb.

There is an old axiom, "Hope for the best but prepare for the worst." That statement should be torqued a bit. The operative word is "prepare," as in "prepare for the best, and prepare for the worst." The leader who can carry in mind as possibilities several scenarios at a time has a great advantage. Often, true wisdom consists not in knowing what to do in the ultimate but in knowing what to do next.

There is a difference, too, between the plan and the action. It's okay to race out to meet problems in your mind, but you don't have to sound general quarters when you construct a scenario that means trouble.

The balancing proverb is "Don't lift your leg till you get to the fence."

If you are going to run with the big dogs, you have to tinkle on tall trees.

The statement, besides being cynical, reveals an unrealistic perception of how the organizational world works best. The belief that only the unscrupulous and the vindictive get ahead is diseased. Not surprisingly, how effective the strategy of attacking senior colleagues is depends on the degree of pathology present in the organization. For the long pull, it's a loser.

Keep a rudder in the water not a paddle.

A good leader must be perceived as having a strong sense of direction, but a leader must delegate. That doesn't mean everyone is a free electron bouncing around each in his or her own random orbit. Delegation requires a shared sense of direction, clear objectives, good communication, trust, shared authority and mutual support. That's a large order. There is no satisfactory alternative if you want people to give their best.

People decide what they want by deciding first what they don't want.

Negotiating out answers from a negative start is part of family living. Why should it be considered a bad technique of leadership if the ultimate objective is to get everyone into the game to achieve a better result?

Illustration:

"Let's go out for Chinese tonight.
Naw, that's too salty.
How about spaghetti?
We had that Monday.
How about . . ."

And the negotiation is on.

Out of this dialectic solutions emerge.

One of the techniques effective leaders sometimes use is to say to a working team, "If you don't tackle me, this is what I am going to do." If people are bright and independent, opposition emerges. Tacklers immediately come onto the field. The pendulum of argument goes back and forth. The end result is often better than the initial proposal.

A part of encouraging this kind of problem solving is that the leader cannot get tied up in his or her underwear. Any solution that prematurely takes up residence in the ego inhibits the process.

"Everybody wants to get to Heaven, nobody wants to die."

TIMING

"If you don't go to people's funerals, they won't go to yours."

-Yogi Berra

There is a difference between impatience and importance.

There is always a backlog. As Terry Paulson reminds us, "You will never ever, ever again in your life be caught up." The most maddening leader to work with is one who is in a frenzy about everything and who, in effect, has no priorities. Remember, other people's priorities may be different from your own and that fact can be critical to results. People actually doing the work should have a say. Including other people in the fixing of the batting order of issues can save a lot of resentment, foot dragging and shoddy performance.

The path of later leads to the
house of never.

Procrastination is an equal opportunity employer. Everyone procrastinates. Delay in arriving at difficult decisions is justified if the delay has some purpose such as to permit further consultation or to test reactions. On the other hand, delays that occur simply because a leader finds a decision difficult are bad news. Unlike fine red wine, some decisions don't get any better with aging. It's true that the person who demands an immediate decision usually has a self-serving agenda that requires deeper inquiry. But, if the delay comes from within and is not part of a reasoned scenario, feel free <u>not</u> to do that. There is bracing wisdom in the African proverb that counsels, "If you're going to swallow a toad, don't look at it too long." Crisp decision making in routine matters can become a habit. Certainly, procrastination can become a way of life. Which comedian was it who once observed, "There was a primitive tribe who had no word for 'no.' Instead they said, 'I'll get around to it.'"?

Grab fortune by the forelock; he is bald behind. — Latin proverb

Remember the millionaire's formula for success, "Rise early, work hard, strike oil."

It's true that to a considerable extent we make our own luck. But it's a humbling and healing perspective to recognize that good fortune has something to do with it. One of the tricks is to recognize good luck and to take advantage of it when it comes by.

As any gambler knows neither good luck nor bad luck lasts forever. The advice to push hard when the pendulum is swinging in your direction and to ease off when everything seems to be going wrong is advice found in Gracian's manual in the 17th century. There really does seem to be a pile-on effect of good or bad events from time to time. "When troubles come, they come not singly but in legions." I read once that in 1895 in the state of Ohio there were only two automobiles, and they had a head-on collision. There is such a thing as "luck."

A college president told me of seeing an ad in a British paper, "Lost, black and white spotted Tom, blind in left eye, missing right ear, partially paralyzed in hind legs, recently castrated, answers to the name of Lucky." Every leader in our society has moments when he or she knows how that cat feels. But that old cat is lucky. Someone still cares enough to advertise, and perhaps we can all boast of that kind of luck.

"The person who says it can't be done shouldn't interfere with the person doing it."

-Old proverb

SURVIVAL

"Sometimes you can't get low enough to see eye to eye."

-Tom Walker

Don't go mountain climbing with your beneficiary.

Unless you're on the western slope in your work and ready to pull the pin, it's usually a bad idea to pick a successor and let that person know it. You can create a sense of caution and concern for the future that can ruin that person's effectiveness and at the same time expose your own caboose. If your successor has already been named and you are crossing the desert together, it might be wise to carry the water bottle.

There is a broader meaning to the proverb. It is usually a bad idea to ask people to execute painful decisions that are clearly against their self-interest if some discretion and skill are required. While most such assignments do not put one in danger of being pushed off a cliff, you're probably not going to get the best and the most wholehearted effort.

If you wouldn't be pleased to see it on the front page of tomorrow's paper, don't do it.

Someone recently commented that these days the TV camera seems to be the weapon with which leaders most frequently commit suicide.

The proverb applies not just to the fact that the world is a whispering gallery, but goes to a matter of inner character and serenity. A leader should never permit herself to reach the point where her mirror becomes an enemy. A commitment to personal integrity gives an inner iron to leaders that is subtly communicated to others. To say that in some ineffable way integrity is critical is as much of an understatement as saying "Quasimodo had poor posture."

The proverb deserves deeper reflection — Our society is now experiencing an awakening concern with ethics and values. Leaders in the near future will be judged as Keepers of the Flame. Shabbiness in personal affairs will be perceived as default in leadership responsibility.

In these times of detailed TV coverage, marquee is important, appearances count. Also, in these days of microscopic investigative reporting, facade is not enough. A leader can be slick enough to slide up hill and still be distrusted.

When history is at a hinge, we expect our leaders to set an example.

The army of Alexander the Great was campaigning in the Middle Eastern desert, and water supplies were exhausted. Alexander's commanders ordered runners to bring water from a distant mountain for their leader. The drink was presented to him in a silver helmet. According to the story, he emptied the water on the sand saying, "I will drink when my soldiers drink."

"There's a time for laughing and a time for not laughing, and this is not one of them."

-Inspector Clouseau

You can't always stay in the shallow end.

Contrary to Norm's warning to Woody in *Cheers*, you can't always "stay in the shallow end."

As they say in baseball, "You can't steal second and keep one foot on first." Was it Francis Bacon who said, "Fortune doth favor the audacious."?

Audacity is absolutely essential for leaders of organizations that are in transition, but it works surprisingly well in stable organizations too. There is a saying in the world of chess, "If you are going to get in the game, move the Queen."

Additionally, an exorbitant thirst to "stay off the skyline" or to make a "low radar signature" is noticed and resented.

If you have to have an answer now, the answer is NO!

When someone comes raging in with his trousers in flames and demands an immediate answer, that person is usually trying, consciously or unconsciously, to bag you. The statement "If you have to have an answer now, the answer is NO!" almost always stretches out the time line and leaves the possibility of looking for fleas wide open. Most problems introduced with a cry for instant action have considerable hair on them.

In the Olympics of leadership, the critical event is not fencing where the lunge takes the point, but weight lifting where you plant your feet and straighten your back before the lift.

If your hair is on fire, don't try to put it out with a hammer.

Sometimes the cure is worse than the disease. Even in crisis situations. I have seen CEO's really escalate crises because, in panic, they lunge at an apocalyptic solution. They either give the place a ground glass enema or else "hoist the black flag and start cutting throats." Often a less drastic remedy would do.

Occasionally, problems work themselves out in which case there is no need to break a butterfly on the rack. In spite of the cries for stronger wine and madder music, "easy does it" is usually the best strategy.

Bedfellows make strange politics.

A happy and monogamous marriage is a wonderful treasure. Not every couple finds it.

Over the years a number of leaders of my acquaintance have gotten themselves in difficulty because of a wandering libido. For highly visible examples, look at national presidents and presidential candidates.

There is a crude locker room proverb, "Never get your meat where you get your bread." Or again, and less bluntly, "Don't fish off the company dock." I've seen leaders, both men and women, seriously compromise their decision making ability because they had established sexual liaisons with people to whom they then had an obligation. If those people were unstable, the problems got out of hand very quickly.

Many times leaders feel that members of the opposite sex admire them simply because of their charm, handsomeness or their beauty. That may not be true. In Western society influence and power are aphrodisiacs. It is often the office that creates the attractiveness, not the wonderfulness of the individual.

Remember, careers can be ruined by sexual boundary violations.

"Today's favor is tomorrow's obligation."

-Bill Wild

There is truth in wine.

Never become over-refreshed. "Agent grape" can be as deadly as "Agent orange." According to a journalist, a famous set of last words in Washington, D.C. is "liquor doesn't affect me." That used to "rank right up there with 'I understand the Russians.'" Liquor is a part of our culture and its misuse is often difficult to identify or label. The leader should remember that it's potentially a very dangerous drug for everyone.

Remember, too, "never forget what people say when they are drunk."

Hansel and Gretel were right.

If Hansel and Gretel were in today's world, they would be leaving memos rather than bread crumbs. In these litigious times it is not a bad idea for leaders and administrators to keep a log of critical events as a hedge against interpretive drift. After all, "Part of the fun of remembering is reinterpreting." One's own record of what went wrong may seem frail support, but I've been present when a somewhat stammering reading from a personal notebook carried the day.

There is another advantage to leaving a paper trail. Having a longer and more consecutive description of events and reactions to those events helps head off tendencies to go in the wrong direction. Yogi Berra once said, "When you come to a fork in the road, take it." The key is to take the right branch.

Too often, memoranda are regarded as the refuge of bureaucrats. The cynical view is that after a short interval all memoranda pass away and go to memorandum heaven and are never heard of again. "Paper blizzards" often mean an organization is unwell.

That admission does not bankrupt a Hansel and Gretel strategy when issues have a fuse.

"It doesn't do to leave a dragon out of your calculations if one lives nearby."

-Tolkien

Rumps in and horns out didn't save the buffalo.

Question: "When things aren't moving or you encounter resistance, the best strategy is to lower your head and charge — right?" Answer: "Usually not." Today's leaders must say grace over a plate that contains delay, obstruction, ambiguity, indecision, and resistance. That's what's on the menu most of the time. The "charge" scenario comes from the belief that there are really no reasons for these problems to exist except inexcusable weakness and human perversity. Organizational problems are more complicated than that. Management is no longer a game of shove if indeed it ever was.

There is a tendency for failing leaders to join the General George A. Custer Memorial Fan Club. The General's strategy of battle "I ride to the sound of the guns" is always heroic, often suicidal. As the old saying goes, "The braver the bird, the fatter the cat."

Don't negotiate when you have to go to the bathroom.

Most historians, if shaken hard enough, will spill out stories of how history was altered because a king or commander had to go to the bathroom at the wrong time. Such stories do not often appear in history books because they are non-canonical and certainly undignified.

There is a lesson to be learned from such reports. Often in negotiations, whether one on one or with a group, some key person picks up the signal that closure is at hand and the meeting almost over. He or she decides to "hold it" for another 30 minutes. People have better antenna than we give them credit for and consciously or unconsciously take advantage of the situation to change the cadence of the meeting from one that promises quick closure to one that gets the slows. A full bladder or bowel pressure are not good companions when important issues are at stake. What is the saying in the diplomatic corps? "Never miss a chance to sit down or go to the bathroom."

Every leader has a few silver bullets.

Once in awhile you have to "go down the path of righteousness like a thunderbolt." Sometimes such actions save the organization, but there is always a price tag. Quick and apocalyptic actions may push back the margins of the clearing, but always in the trees, waiting, are the quick eyes and the sharp teeth. That means you must choose your issues carefully. Pick a set of regrets with which you are willing to live. Choose carefully the hill on which you are willing to die.

Don't let someone else learn to shave on your beard.

It is a male but not a sexist statement. Be cautious when colleagues reporting to you demand that they be permitted to "do it my own way" if you are the one who has to sweep up after the elephant. If you know a course of action is bad judgment, where colleagues are only going to get stuck on the fly paper, it is well to head the plan off before rather than after the fact. Letting people launch into Ralph Kramden schemes under the banner of learning from their mistakes is bad judgment. We usually don't learn from such experiences. There is always someone else to blame when the solar powered flashlight idea bombs. It's often the leader who is left standing around in his shorts.

This advice has nothing to do with responsible delegation.

When they're after you, they're after you.

Did you hear about the guy who spent $5,000 to cure his bad breath and then found out people didn't like him anyway?

An administrator always rides the mechanical bull. Leaders are always standing on the trap door. Every leader flies his kite in thunder — is always at risk. What did Churchill say? "We live under a drizzle of constant criticism."

The mumbling may become mutinous. Perhaps, time has run out as it sometimes does for leaders. There has been no change in leadership but a change in followership.

Even though the lights are dim in this area, many leaders probably leave Dodge City too soon.

Remember when times get better, the reputations of leaders gets better.

Then the question remains, what do you do when someone continually wets on your leg? What is the best way to handle attack? Is counter attack the best move? Does a soft answer turn away wrath? Is humor a good approach? The evidence simply isn't in. Consult with knowledgeable and impartial colleagues as much as possible which means expanding the network of people with whom you work. Then do what seems wise and fits your personal style.

"A 'nice doggie' tone of voice only works with nice doggies."

-Dick Childs

COMMUNICATION

"Human beings developed speech out of a deep genetic need to complain."

-Lily Tomlin

Don't give cashmere answers to
burlap questions.

Cultivate the habit of plain, straight talk. You don't have to be rude, you don't have to be shrill, just be straight. Plain talk can often be gently given, "Soft were his words, but be they very swords." Communication is the sometimes thin and uncertain cement that holds us together.

A word of caution. Straight talk doesn't mean you have to throw up on everyone. How does the old saying go, "You should always tell the truth, but the whole truth does not always need to be told." That may seem equivocal but it isn't if you capture the spirit.

Sticks and stones can break your bones, but words can do permanent damage. — Movie Disk Jockey

Try to keep your foot out of your mouth. Toes taste terrible. Saying the wrong thing at the wrong time is often related to the habit of recreational bitching. As the wise Chinese proverb advises, "Keep your broken arm inside your sleeve."

"When you get to the place where you are beginning to take your complaints seriously, get another job."

This advice is not just a matter of political wisdom for the individual. Constant complaining affects the functioning of the organization. Recreational bitching and bad mouthing of colleagues spreads and subtly creates a climate in which dreams die and warm personal relationships deteriorate.

Truth lives at the bottom of the well.

The truth is never pure and seldom simple. Events in organizations are always complicated. The advice "never believe anything that is whispered," or "always search for someone with an alternate point of view," or "never believe the first version that you hear" are sound counsel. As someone has commented, "You are smart if you believe only half of what you hear, you're a genius if you know which half to believe."

No one acts as tough as he talks.

People often over read a statement of understanding, sympathy or concern coming from a leader. They translate such an interchange into a conviction that the leader has promised full scale war on their behalf.

Such misunderstandings are related to the smaller confusions originating around the water cooler. "Sure, I'll go down and talk to accounting. They can't treat you like that. I'll give them hell." Often the later actions seem a little watery to the person who has been promised support if he or she is in on the conversation that is expected to fulfill the promise.

Someone once remarked, "Everyone wants a strong leader by which they mean someone who will pursue their pet objectives ruthlessly."

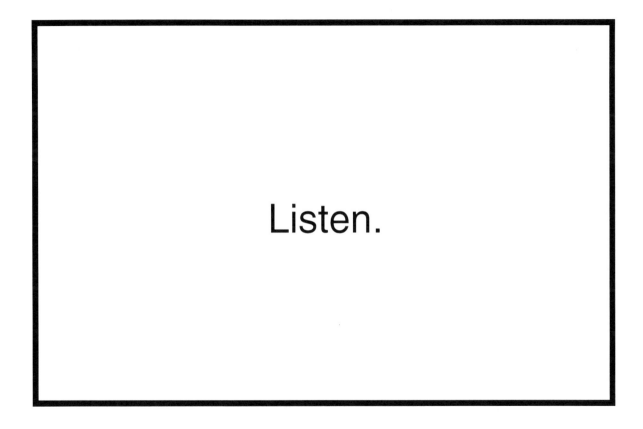

Listen.

Leaders are often articulate, sometimes even compulsive talkers. The characteristic is noted in such statements as, "No one ever got hoarse in a conversation with Smith." Or, "A monk once broke a vow of silence to tell him to shut up." Good communication is vital for leaders. Listening is a critical part of good communication.

I remember a cartoon showing two bank-type windows with bars. Over one there is a sign 'Teller' with no one waiting to be served. The other window has a sign over it 'Listener' and a long line.

One of the qualities for which good leaders always receive compliments is that of being a good listener. Everyone needs to talk. Everyone needs to be witnessed. Everyone needs to be attended to. We need to be heard in order to metabolize experience.

Listening involves hearing the unspoken message as well as the nouns and verbs. Learn to understand the full message behind the rhetoric. It's harder than it sounds.

Confidential is something that you discuss with one person at a time.

Benjamin Franklin said it, "Three can keep a secret if two are dead." Organizations are whispering galleries. If people don't have information, they make it up. When gossip spreads through an organization, it's like tearing a pillow in the wind. You never get all the feathers back. We are vastly communicative.

That fact can sometimes be turned to an advantage. If someone is pooping off, a little judicious worry with a friend of the individual involved can often solve a problem. "Don't tell Grumblewhack, but I'm concerned about the tardiness of the last two assignments. Don't mention it. It's not even worth talking about yet. . ." can be more effective than a direct confrontation.

Additional counsel is in order. Never give an important message to just one person. Shorten the lines and talk to several people throughout the organization.

This is a process that computer networks will not only make easier but inevitable. The view that the way to communicate is to tell only the people who report to you and depend on them in turn to tell their subordinates doesn't work well. To "feed the sparrows by feeding the horses" is not a sound strategy. It is especially unrealistic in these days of "wired" organizations where everyone has a computer.

"There's nothing as frustrating as the pain of an unmade speech."

There is a difference between a horse chestnut and a chestnut horse.

How things are said is important. Words count.

The first general application of this proverb is, "don't say too much." Sometimes even one word can be too many. As Robert Benchley reminds us, "One, two, three, buckle my shoe" doesn't make it. There is only one extra word, but as Mark Twain once observed, "The difference between a lightning bug and lightning is considerable."

A second meaning to this proverb is that the way things are said is crucial. I once read that tuna fish was first marketed under the name of "horse mackerel." Needless to say, sales records weren't broken.

Another illustration. Once upon a time, I lived in a community where two health spas opened at the same time. One advertised, "Lose your ugly fat." The other advertised, "Keep your trim figure." You guess which one is still open.

Bear in mind that people can be pulled better than they can be pushed. Advice can be presented as though the other person had already suggested it.

Also, when a mistake has been made, it sometimes helps if the boss can assign part of the blame to him or herself. "My directions may not have been clear, I apologize." It changes nothing but is immensely healing.

"Be careful not to speak more clearly than you're thinking."

-Adapted from old political joke

PERCEPTIONS

"Unless you know what it is, I ain't never gonna be able to explain it to ya."

-Louis Armstrong on jazz

We see only what we look for.
We look for only what we know.

One of the great cancer surgeons of our time at the Harvard Medical School had this proverb written on cardboard and placed in the corner of a bookcase near his desk where he, not the patient, could see it. The proverb could have continued with the observation that we can "know" only what we understand, and we understand only what we can connect with other experience.

It was once my privilege to hear Francis Crick of DNA fame give a brilliant lecture. In the course of his remarks, he pointed out that all of us must organize experience in order to function in the world. He said, "If the front door of this room should suddenly burst open and a clown with a pitchfork appear and then a few seconds later a back door open and an alligator waddle in, everyone here would be constructing a scenario to connect those events."

Leaders should be careful of the stories they tell themselves. Scenarios that are full of suspicion, themes inhabited by gloomy and lugubrious imaginings are bad news.

Be realistic, be sunny and try not to go too far beyond the facts. Often problems that seem hopeless can be solved with a different strategy. Usually those working with you on a team are not out to "get" you or to embarrass you. The unsuspicious, self-confidence of the leader pulls others along to the summit.

"We believe that we may know."

-Augustine

Enter houses through their doors.

This old Bedouin proverb counsels the fundamental wisdom and fairness of accepting people at face value. The proverb, insofar as it warns against imputing motivation to people, is exceedingly wise and timely. Most of the difficulty in organizations begins with mutterings such as "I know what he's trying to do, he's trying to set me up." Or "She wants to make me look bad to protect her own back bumper." We are heroes in our own eyes, and though we want to be judged on our motives, we tend to judge others by their actions, or our perceptions of their actions. One of the best ways to get people to behave in a fair and high-hearted fashion is to treat them as though they were already doing so.

It is better to trust too much than too little.

That piece of wisdom goes back in history. Hear it again. In the organizational environments of today almost anything will work if the people involved trust one another. If trust is absent, nothing works. This statement has even greater meaning in the widely dispersed, closely wired large organizations on the tender growing edge of change. Close supervision is less possible. Nurturing and vision building skills are at once more necessary and more difficult to apply. The treasure of trust must continually be created and re-created.

Trust must begin with the leader, but that isn't always easy. The leader who first discovers that his or her position attracts a certain amount of hostility and suspicion is going to have a reaction of caution and surprise. There will be an impulse to hunt for villains. That's normal. It takes a while for leaders to build up a realistic picture of the rules for political behavior. But the leader who comes to see him or herself as a "Klingon starship with the shields up" is, as the kids say, "seriously weird."

We're standing on the edge of an abscess. —Sam Goldwyn

In these days gloom and doom are in good supply. There's a bumper sticker around that reads, "The meek are contesting the will."

A comment of W. C. Fields is also understandable. According to the story, when his doctor told him his heavy drinking was damaging his auditory nerve, Fields replied, "Well, Doc, what I've been drinking is a lot better than what I've been hearing."

We feel faintly guilty about our sunnier hopes and dreams. Despair is more politically correct.

According to legend when Satan was cast from the battlements of heaven, one of his fellow rebel angels asked him what he missed most about Paradise and he replied, "The sound of trumpets in the morning." We need hope. We need optimism. We need the sound of trumpets.

As someone reminds us, "We're all like spaghetti, it's easier to pull us than to push us."

There are big battalions behind pessimism, but it won't sustain the leader and his or her organization. Optimism is the thyroid gland of democracy. But more than that, no successful leader of my memory or acquaintance has been a pessimist. They have all been optimists or closet optimists. Alan Lerner, of the team of Lerner and Lowe, spoke for most when he said, "I no longer believe in miracles. I've seen too many of them."

A pessimist is more than just "an optimist who has been mugged," but the hard evidence for pessimism, put in historic perspective, is not as sturdy as it seems. Pessimism is a state of mind. We now suffer from what Chopin referred to as "Englishman's disease." We play the good notes with indifference and the bad notes with great feeling.

Mike Todd, the famous movie producer, once answered a question at a Hollywood party, "Have you ever been poor?" with the answer, "No, of course not." A friend whirled on him and said, "Mike, what are you talking about? I've known you when you didn't have one dime to rub against another." Todd replied, "Oh, no, that's being broke. I've been broke lots of times. Being broke is a temporary state of affairs. Being poor is a state of mind."

The historical record shows there are good reasons to be optimistic. Gaudy forecasts of doom are being "recalled like defective cars." This doesn't mean that we should be ruthlessly glad about everything that goes on in our country today, but in perspective, as a nation, we have considerable reason to be optimistic.

We're making the melting pot idea work pretty well. On balance and in the long term, we're making our pluralism a plus rather than a minus.

When we look at other countries in the world, we realize how startling the melting pot idea is and how effectively it works compared with the alternative.

We have the best universities in the world and the best researchers.

We have not yet solved the problem of health care for everyone, but our cutting edge medicine is the best in the world.

We're the strongest military power.

The whole world emulates American culture, its pop music, its Levis, its movies, television and its fashions.

We're living longer than our parents and far longer than our grandparents.

There are occasional hints in the Environmental Protection Agencies data and in the research findings of other groups that our environment is getting cleaner not dirtier.

Compared to a hundred years ago, our crime rate is lower, and our use of drugs is less.

We still have a strong and noticeable sense of traditional values.

It is not fashionable to say so, but all in all the progress we are making is cause for hope not despair, optimism rather than gloom. Social change is occurring at such a pace that we may well be in the morning of a new world.

More than that, democracy is a self-cleaning oven, we can and do correct our mistakes. The pendulum swings from excess to excess but settles closer to the middle.

Finally, as Eric Sevaried has said, "The world still turns our way because of the strength of our most decent ideals."

I like what Cesar Chavez, leader of the United Farm Workers, once said, "You know what I think? I really think that one day the world will be great. I really believe the world gonna be great one day."

"Somewhere, just out of sight, great things are moving."

-Theodore White

Acknowledgements

I am indebted to legions of friends, colleagues and acquaintances for virtually everything I know, the rest I have learned from landing on my head. Am I the original author of all the one liners in this book? Certainly not. A sound percentage, it's true are either mine or came to me through my father, grandfather or my brother. All of whom were, on occasion, verbal cartoonists.

I'm grateful to everyone who contributed to the one liners in this book whether that is a contribution of which I am aware or not is certainly true that "All of us are smarter than any of us."

Thanks to TIME magazine for permission to use quoted material.

"If you ain't used to a whole lot, this may not be too bad."

-Walt Garrison

Adam and Eve 42
Adversary 127, 128
African proverb 148
Alda, Alan 92
Alexander the Great 159
Allah 41
Allen, Woody 99
American Cancer Society . . 46
Anger 52, 107, 108, 120
Annoyances 48
Apathy 16
Aphrodisiacs 169
Apple 56
Approval 36, 46
Armstrong, Louis 210
Army 56, 86, 94, 159
Assembly line 18
Augustine 214
Back-up lights 131
Backlog 146

Bacon 162
Bad luck 150
Bad mouthing 194
Ball player 15
Barney Miller Show 119
Baseball 16, 35, 162
Bathroom 179, 180
Bedfellows 167
Bedpan 95
Beginner 20
Believe 214
Benchley, Robert 206
Beneficiary 155
Berra, Yogi 144, 174
Big dogs 135
Bird 178
Black flag 166
Brown, Charlie 90
Bubble up 17
Buffalo 177

Bunker, Archie 97
Bureaucracy 64
Burlap questions 191
Butterfly 100, 166
Cashmere answers 191
Cat 151, 178
Caterpillar 100
Caught up 146
CEO 50, 72, 90, 166
Chain of command 32,
. . . . 36, 62
Chavez, Cesar 225
Cheers 162
Childs, Dick 188
Chili 56
Chinese proverb 108,
. . . . 130, 194
Chopin 221
Christopher Robin 14
Churchill 186

Cigar 24
Climates 30
Commanders 56, 84, 159
Committee 75, 76
Committees 76, 77
Common sense 12
Communication 72,
. . . . 138, 189, 192, 200
Complain 190
Compliment 82, 89, 90
Computer 84, 203
Confidential 201
Consent 36
Cookie 84
Cooper, Gary 56
Coward 128
CPA 54
Credit, who receives 77,
. . . . 79, 81, 82, 180
Crick, Francis 212
Crime 224
Criticism 88,
. . . . 90, 104, 106, 186

Custer, George A. 178
Daedalus 91
Damn fool 101
de Tocqueville, Alex 96
Debit column 53, 54
Delegate 138
Democracies 38
Democracy 24, 221, 224
Detective Sergeant Fish . . 119
Dialectic solutions 140
Dictators 32
Die 142, 182, 194
DNA 212
Dodge City 186
Dog 73, 97, 110
Dogs 66, 135
Dr. Ruth 26
Dragon 176
Drugs 224
Edward Bear 14
Elephant 184
Eleventh commandment . . 30
Emerson, Ralph Waldo . . 116

Enemy 106, 122, 158
Evil 31
Expert 20
Eye to eye 154
Fair play 32
Favor 162, 170
Fear 31, 32
Fencing 164
Fields, W. C. 220
Financial expertise 54
Flattery 49
Fleas 100, 164
Flower garden 30
Fonzie Bear 96
Forgiveness 80
Fortune 149, 150, 162
Franklin, Benjamin 202
Freedom 18, 71, 72
Friends 46, 94, 122, 227
Front page 157
Frontier rhyme 122
Frost, Robert 34
Frustration 120

Funeral 104, 112
Garrison, Walt 67, 228
Genes 12
God 75, 102, 133
Goldwyn, Sam 219
Gomez, Lefty 68
Good intentions 109, 120
Good luck 150
Gossip 202
Gracian's Manual 150
Grape 96, 172
Great things 226
Gun 56, 108
Guns 178
Hammer 17, 165
Hammer down 17
Hansel and Gretel . . . 173-175
Happiness 29
Hardball 96
Harvard Medical School . . 212
Heart 16, 24, 26, 92, 113
Heaven 42, 142, 175, 220
Hell 16, 42, 109, 198

History . . 32, 84, 159, 180, 218
Hope 46,
. . . . . 52, 103, 134, 220, 224
Horses 124, 203
Hubris 28
Human beings . . . 48, 126, 190
Icarus 91
Image 110
Impatience 145
Importance 145
Incoming traffic 47
Indignation 130
Inspector Clouseau 160
Jackass 52
Jazz 210
Juggler 70
Keepers of the Flame 158
Kennedy, John F. 83
Kill . . . 52, 56, 60, 94, 105, 128
Kings 106
KMA 57
Kramden, Ralph 184
Later 147, 198, 212

Laughing 50, 160
Law, Vernon 15
Lawrence, Bob 80
Lawyers 99
Learning disability 27
Lerner, Alan 221
Les Miserables 97
Levant, Oscar 94
Libido 168
Liquor 172
Listen 199
Lombardi, Vince 66
Longsworth, Alice Roosevelt
. . . . 34
Loren, Sophia 40
Lowe 221
Loyalty 32
Luck 150, 151
Machiavellian 91, 114
Mad 96, 100
March, Jim 97
Mayo Clinic 18
Mead, Margaret 133

Medication 52
Melting pot 222, 223
Memorandum 175
Memos 174
Messenger 105, 106
Middle East 42
Millionaire 150
Milne, A. A. 14
Minerva 33, 34
Miss Piggy 55, 56
Monkey 78, 130
Morale 38, 68, 114
Motives 110, 216
Mountain 155, 159
Moving 22, 121, 178, 226
Mr. Rogers' Neighborhood
. . . . 118
Murders 117, 118
Negotiate 179
Negotiating 140
Nelson, Willie 67
Neurons 12
Nice doggie 188

Nice guys 25
Obedience 71, 72, 126
Obedience school 126
Obligation 168, 170
Olympics of leadership . . . 164
Optimism 220, 221, 224
Owl 33, 34
Oz 26
Paddle 137
Path of retreat 127
Paulson, Terry 146
Peanuts 44
Perceptions 209, 216
Perfume 49
Permission 80
Person doing it 152
Pessimism 221
Physicians 63
Pinata 52
Pittsburgh Pirates 15
Play hurt 98
Poet 68
Pogo 28

Poker 113, 114
Political 37, 194, 208
Political behavior 36, 218
Political joke 208
Politics 35, 167
Pooh 12, 14
Popcorn 44
Power 36, 90, 169, 223
Praise 60, 82, 88
Prepare 133, 134
President 42, 46
. . . . 50, 54, 62, 91, 151
Pretend 64
Pro football 98
Procrastination 148
Puppy 46
Pyramid 19, 72
Queen 162
Raisin 96
Religions 24
Remember 59, 60
Resentments 120, 121
Respect 46

Revenge 100, 128
Rudder 34, 137
Russians 172
Salary 88
Saltzman, Paul 16
Satan 220
Scoundrels 118
Secret 34,
.... 56, 68, 84, 202
Sergeant Preston of the Yukon
.... 73
Sevaried, Eric 225
Sexual boundary violations
.... 169
Shallow end 161, 162
Shave 183
Shouting match 101
Silver bullets 181
Sinsheimer, Robert 12
Skunks 69
Smart ass 51, 52
Snake farm 21, 22
Solomon 54

Solution 43, 44, 141, 166
Solve problems 30, 44, 63
Songs 67, 116
Speech 114, 190, 204
State Department 86
Sticks and stones 193
Stories 120, 121, 180, 213
Straight talk 192
Strangers 94
Strong leader 198
Student radicals 86
Success group 84
Successor 156
Suicide 158
Supervisor 36, 96
Surgeon 88
Tacklers 141
Talent 18, 63, 70, 90
Tantrum 102
Tarzans 37
Teams 18, 37, 68,
.... 70, 73, 74, 77, 106
Teamwork 32

Television 24, 86, 223
Temper 102, 110
Temper tantrum 102
Thinking 208
Thousand friends 122
Thunderbolt 182
Toad 148
Today's favor 170
Todd, Mike 222
Tolkien 176
Tomlin, Lily 190
Tough 76, 97, 132, 197
Tree 37, 97
Trial ballooning 22
Trust 41, 138, 217, 218
Truth 52, 116,
.... 171, 192, 195, 196
TV 158, 159
Twain, Mark 206
Tyrants 96, 114
Universe 100
Unmade speech 204
Unreasonable people 129

Vacillation 132
Values 30, 158, 224
Victory 83, 84
Villain 62, 63, 118
Villains 84, 86, 218
Volleyball 74
Walker, Ed 124
Walker, Tom 154

War 107, 198
Washington, D.C. 90, 172
Wayne, John 132
Weapons 86
Weber, Max 72
Weight lifting 164
Wild, Bill 170
Wilson, Flip 78

Wilson, Woodrow 72
Wine 148, 166, 171
Winnie-the-Pooh 14
Wisdom 34, 54, 90, 100,
. . . . . . 134, 148, 194, 216, 218
Work force 18, 34
Worker 18, 96
Zen 20

234

About the Author

The author is a nationally recognized speaker and lecturer in the fields of management, leadership and university administration. He has been president of three universities and chancellor of a community college district, has served on hospital boards, national commissions and has testified before the Appropriations Committee of the Congress of the United States. His widely used text *The Effective Administrator*, published by Jossey-Bass is in its 6th printing.

Walker holds a bachelor's degree (summa cum laude) and a master's degree from the University of Southern California and a doctoral degree in sociology from Stanford University. He is a licensed psychologist in the State of California and the Commonwealth of Massachusetts.

ORDER FORM

Please send _____ copy(ies) of *"Never Try to Teach a Pig to Sing...": Wit & Wisdom for Leaders* @ $12.95 each, $13.95 to California addresses (includes tax). I understand that if, for any reason, I am not satisfied, I may return this book for a full refund.

Shipping: Book rate $2.50 for first book and $1.00 for each additional book.

Fax orders: (619) 462-5737

Telephone orders: (619) 589-6608. Have your VISA or MasterCard ready.

Postal orders: Lathrop Press, P.O. Box 19306-1, San Diego, CA 92159-0306

Name: _____

Address: _____

City: _____ State: _____ Zip: _____

Payment: ☐ Check   ☐ Credit Card   ☐ VISA   ☐ MasterCard

Card Number: _____ Exp. Date: _____

Signature: _____

ORDER FORM

Please send _____ copy(ies) of *"Never Try to Teach a Pig to Sing...": Wit & Wisdom for Leaders* @ $12.95 each, $13.95 to California addresses (includes tax). I understand that if, for any reason, I am not satisfied, I may return this book for a full refund.

Shipping: Book rate $2.50 for first book and $1.00 for each additional book.

Fax orders: (619) 462-5737

Telephone orders: (619) 589-6608. Have your VISA or MasterCard ready.

Postal orders: Lathrop Press, P.O. Box 19306-1, San Diego, CA 92159-0306

Name: _____

Address: _____

City: _____ State: _____ Zip: _____

Payment: ☐ Check   ☐ Credit Card   ☐ VISA   ☐ MasterCard

Card Number: _____   Exp. Date: _____

Signature: _____